Forget what was start anew

You can't change the past
But the future is yours.

CARLOS MATEO

An improbable true story that Otto told me one a long night

Introduction

Otto tells how it came about:"On my last trip to Europe, I had some things to do, I wanted to sell my house, the furniture and also my much loved car. It was a hard farewell, 40 years we lived in this place and in this house and now other owners are using my things. They live in my house, which we saved from our mouths. The biggest part of building the house I did myself. We had no vacation, every free minute I worked on building the house. Then came the children, again no free minute.

At Christmas, we bought a small dog for the children, there was great joy. Gradually, we were financially better, and we bought a used car on installments, also the TV, of course in color, that was an expensive matter at that time in the 60s, was bought on installments. It was a difficult time, but we held together, it was only bought cheaply or better cheaply, and it was saved behind and in front. Then the children came to school, we lived in a village which at that time had about 800 inhabitants. Today there are about 25,000 inhabitants, with banks, supermarket, shopping center, cinema, municipal swimming pool, etc.

We were not rich, but happy, and I think that was the most important thing. Later the children left home, they started their families and we 2 were alone. But I still wanted to tell my story, although the above is also part of my story. On my last visit, I was alone and the evenings are very long, you long for a beer or a glass of wine. Well, I went to a bar and since all the seats were taken, the waiter seated me at a table with a gentleman. We got acquainted, as we were taught to do when we were kids. His name was Carlos, and we got to talking, and I brought it upon myself to tell my whole life story. Carlos asked me at the end of our conversation if he could write it down, he told me he was a writer and my narrative inspired him."

When Otto came into the world, in 1937, there was a wartime atmosphere in the country and World War 2 was coming. Well, he was still too young to know anything about it, his parents lived with him in a big Bavarian city. His father worked there as a designer for engines.

Otto was I think, about 75 years, we were immediately sympathetic and Otto began to tell. What I got to hear was a whole life with all its ups and downs.

His fate was so interesting, I had never heard anything like it before. Thinking back now, I heard a whole life that night. It was pure coincidence or was it fated that we met that night. We sat together all night, talking and talking. In my mind I asked myself, why is he telling me all this.

At first, I thought he was just telling me a fairy tale, but then I realized that something was being told here that was true, and Otto had to get it all off his chest. This night with me was supposed to help Otto talk about his problems and find a way to lead a better life, even if he only had a short time left until the end.

Otto was a bit excited when he started to talk, he was a so-called grown man. He started, which was strange, with his childhood and told me a whole period of at least 70 years. I admire the memory of Otto, he told and told.

When we both separated in the early morning, I felt a relief in Otto, he had processed all the garbage, it was already a pile of garbage or better, a landfill Otto talked off his chest.

Again and again I put off writing all this down, I had other things to do, but now I will write this story down because Otto's life is worth writing about.

Here you can read a true improbable story, a story that life wrote.

How it all began with Otto,
he told it all

I, Otto was born in 1937 in Cologne on the Rhine, my father worked as an engineer in a company that manufactured engines. But my father didn't want to stay in Cologne, he was from Thuringia, and he was drawn to the south of Germany. He applied to several companies and got a job as an engine designer in a company in Franconia. Our little family moved away from Cologne, and we started a new life in Franconia. Just to remind you, I made his first train trip with my mother from Cologne to Thuringia when I was 3 weeks old, that was just by the way, it was my first visit, to my grandparents.

I was about four years old and grew up in a big city. The war came also to Bavaria, flight alarm and off into the cellars, one night was again flight alarm and the inhabitants of the whole house ran into the air-raid shelter. It was a terrible attack, even in the air-raid shelter vibrations were felt, and I had terrible fear, which accompanied me almost my whole life. Everyone in the cellar felt that death was quite near, and it was pure luck that no bombs hit this house.

When the all-clear came, oh horror, our apartment was a pure pile of rubble. Windows were broken, the doors were off their hinges, all the furniture was heavily occupied, it was no longer possible to live in this apartment. My father got emergency accommodation from his company, in which we could live to some extent. Because of this and the constant attacks, my parents decided that my mother and I would go to my grandparents' house to be somewhat safe from the bad attacks. After all, it was safer in the village than in the city. So, I came to the small village in Thuringia.

In the middle of the preparations for the trip came the next blow, my father was drafted into the military. We arrived after a long train journey, the train had to stop several times because air raids were reported on the route, at the small station 10 km from the village and my grandfather picked us up there with his horse-drawn carriage. So, Otto moved into the small village, it had about 500 inhabitants, on the border with Bavaria. The war was everywhere. At the age of 6 I entered the local elementary school, a small village school with 2 classrooms for 1 - 4 and 5 - 8.

It was not easy for me, school did not cause me any problems. But there is always something that creates turmoil in a quiet life. So, it was with me, I was afraid, when I heard an airplane, I immediately threw myself in the dirt, my classmates teased me, and sometimes I was attacked".

The little one persevered, he took everything, one day was again an attack on him, he was lucky and hit the worst and strongest of all the children directly on the nose, so the blood splashed and the feared by all tore out.

"I had become braver from one moment to the next and from then on, I was respected and my life became calmer. That's how it is sometimes in life. Call it what you will, I think here heaven has helped"

"Life in the countryside was less dangerous, but my nerves were badly battered, my victor in the schoolyard helped me to become braver and freer. I was a good student and always brought home good grades to the delight of my mother."

"One day the war was almost over and we boys were playing in the forest as usual, there were many weapons lying around that the German soldiers had thrown away and we children were collecting them. The Americans were already quite close, we found a bazooka in the forest. One of the bigger boys said, I know how this thing works, we just need a string and have to hide in the holes dug by the soldiers, then we'll try it out. No sooner said than done, the big boy attached the string and all the kids hid in the holes they had dug. Then a hiss and a crash, trees were bent or broken off and the thing was fascinating for us. What came next was less beautiful because at the same moment the forest was shelled. The Americans were already all around. All of us were hiding in holes, fortunately we were not hit. But the smell that came out of those foxholes was terrible.

But then everything got worse, the American soldiers searched the forest and found us in the holes. We were scared to death because these soldiers were blacks, and they eat little children as it was always propagated. Now it was finally over for us. But the soldiers laughed when they saw us and pulled us out of the holes, cleaned us up and gave us chocolate, oranges and bananas to eat. We didn't know all this, we were afraid at the beginning, it is poisoned what we get, but the soldiers ate it too because there was no such thing to buy in the war. We tasted and then we ate everything".

The soldiers put us on a tank and drove us to the small village". Otto said, "we were the first to have contact with the occupation and took the village with us. So, we came home, our parents were distressed, because they knew we were in the forest."

"Later I went to my other grandparents in the mill, I was now no longer afraid of the American soldiers. They all knew me already". "When I came to my grandparents' farm," Otto said, "there was a jeep with soldiers, and they had an interpreter with them who wanted to clarify it for my grandfather that he had to vacate his house within 12 hours because the Americans wanted it as headquarters."

"But they didn't know my grandmother yet, who was listening to everything in the house. She came to the front door and started talking to the soldiers in American, or better yet, Texan because she had grown up with her parents in Galveston, Texas. All the soldiers stood in the yard with their mouths open and the chief of you then said to my grandmother, Mam you don't have to leave, you are one of us after all" Otto told.

"A little later the commander came and asked my grandmother if the Americans could not cook and eat in the house for the officers, and she had no work, everything is done and the whole family could then also with food."

"So a few months passed, and I was a lot with the Americans, I also learned a little English, and so I could communicate a little."

"One day the Americans left and the Russians came. It is sufficiently known how it was then. My other grandparents, where I also lived with my mother, were the first residence in the small village, and they received quartering from a Russian officer. Lucky for the grandparents, one day a Russian came, drunk and started to get violent. At that moment the officer came and the Russian was arrested. They then punished him very harshly later, we could hear the screaming from him".

What happened next?

"School started again, we had gotten a teacher who was a cobbler and had no idea about school. This also passed and after some time the situation normalized and two teachers came who then taught all of us. After 8 years of school was over, my parents, my father was meanwhile back from war or from captivity, wanted me to attend high school and do my Abitur. Unfortunately, this was not possible because my parents were capitalists and higher education was only possible for workers' children.

So I learned agriculture. When I was 14 years old, I joined acquaintances on a big farm to learn, it was not made easy for me, I had to do the same heavy work as the other helpers, despite my 14 years. But this helped me to become more independent and to look at life from a different point of view.

After 10 months it was over, I had to go home, my maternal grandparents were taken away by the Russians and nobody knew if my parents and I would be taken as well.

It was not at that, and I learned still 1 year on the yard of my grandparents. The teacher of the vocational school had told my father to register me at the agricultural technical school, it was about 20 km away from the village.

No sooner said than done and I was accepted. In September, life began at the boarding school of the "Hochschule for Agriculture".

It must have been a wonderful time, Otto raved about this boarding school. He told me he learned a lot that year. With the school, he went on vacation to the island of Rügen, it was a great experience for him. Him.the students formed groups. In this vacation, the nights were longer than the days and everything was a huge fun.

"At harvest time, it was so common or mandatory that all students of agricultural colleges had to help with the duck. We were taken by bus to various cooperatives, and we had to work hard. We slept on straw in an old glue factory, which we were not used to, but it was a lot of fun.

The food wasn't great, but we all organized something, and so we had plenty to eat."

"As it happens, my father got an offer from his old job in the big city in Bavaria to work in his profession again, and he couldn't refuse. So, my technical school time came to an end after one year."

However, it was practically impossible to move legally to the West, a friend of a father had found out in the constitution that it said, everyone can take his residence where he wants. This was the reason to apply for and get an exit permit. It was a stony and long way, but it was successful.

Meanwhile, I had found a job at the tractor station in town and worked with a small tractor in the fields.

In the neighboring town, right on the state border was often a cinema and almost all the youth from the village went the 4 km to the cinema, since we lived close to the border with Bavaria, was of course, as today also by the virus, curfew. At 10 in the evening it was over, but on this evening it had snowed and we boys made a great snowball fight. As it happens, the police came and because the curfew had passed, we were all arrested and sent to the local jail. Until 6 in the morning we were locked up, then we could all leave.

In December of the same year, the time had come, my father and I were given the exit permit, and we had 24 hours to leave the country. We took a cab to the train station and after the checks were over, we started our journey. After about 1 hour we passed the border of Bavaria and a new life began or should begin, my father and I really puffed up.

A new life begins

"The new life began, we arrived in the city and the company of my father had provided a company apartment. I was almost 18 years came to a new environment, actually I should know it, I had been there as a child, since I was still small, I did not remember. The people spoke a different dialect, and it sounds strange, but communication within the German lands was somewhat difficult. When I came to the village then, I spoke this dialect and the communication was funny, and now was the same again. All the traffic, cars, streetcars and lots of people, made me nervous."

"My father was looking for connections for me, so I could settle in better, and he got in touch with a gentleman who directed a chamber choir. That's how I became a singer. I enjoyed that a lot. The choir was well known and had a good name. The whole choir went to a music festival in Stuttgart, where many choirs from Germany performed their songs, and the chamber choir contributed to the festival with the world premiere of Carmina Burana by Carl Orff.

The most prominent audience member in the hall was German President Theodor Heuss, who shook hands with all the singers from the Chamber Choir at the e "Singer was nice, but I always had empty pockets. Since I was used to working, I looked for some kind of work and found an ad in the newspaper, an advertiser wanted for the newspaper.

I applied and got the job. The pay was: commission for each subscription sold and 20 marks per day. For a whole week, I went from house to house in the villages, unsuccessfully.

With my dialect, I was difficult to understand and people did not order anything. What was the end, I flew out as a canvasser, but got 20 marks for that week for each day. My first earned a hundred, I was proud to have so much money.

"In the daily newspaper I found an ad, a gas station was looking for a car washer. I don't remember what they wanted to pay. Car washing was backbreaking work, washing everything manually and then polishing it. I started but no one told me how to do it and what all to wash, so I started, it also only lasted a week, then it was over there too."

"There was a similar agricultural college, my father said I could continue my studies there. But I was rejected, what I had learned didn't fit into the program of that school. I think my dialect did not fit".

"So I kept looking and one day I found an ad, an apprentice wanted in an electrical wholesaler. So, I went and applied, working 6 days a week. They paid 40 marks a month the first year, but I didn't care, I then had a steady job and could continue studying if I wanted. This was a small company, a married couple with a son and 2 daughters.

They sold mixers at fairs all over Germany and the first thing I had to do was get my driver's license 3 because none of the family had a license anymore, it was taken away from them because they drove drunk. I didn't think bad, I got the license for free.

After that, I was on the road all over Germany, setting up trade show booths, delivering and then back to the office. It went well for 1 year, then they went bankrupt, and I was back on the street.

Meanwhile, my language had improved and an acquaintance told me that they were looking for apprentices in a real electrical wholesalerI went there and started right away. Since I had already finished the first year, I started the second year there.

My salary was already princely, 100 Marks a month. Then I studied for another 2 years and took my final exams. Besides, I had a job in a travel agency as a travel companion. Every weekend in summer we went by bus to Austria and in winter to South Tyrol. He got some pay for each trip and the travel guests also gave a small tip, which I shared with the chauffeur."

"After my apprenticeship, I worked in various companies in the city and then went to the capital to an electrical wholesaler as a salesman. Here I earned good money, attended the DAG evening university and studied business administration. As life goes, I met a girl, fell in love, and we got married.

It was a good marriage, we had 2 boys and I got a good job in Italy as an export clerk, I was paid decently. My family lived in Germany, I had bought us a house, and so I always went to Italy on Monday morning at 3 o'clock and on Saturday I came back."

"My family and I were doing well, and we were happy, I was satisfied with my work and the company also appreciated me. So, as a Christmas gift for my wife and me, we got a plane ticket to New York, a hotel voucher for 10 days and the necessary pocket money.

Time passed quickly and after a few years I started my own business in Germany, selling the company's products and adding other companies. It went splendidly, and I thought, Otto, now you have provided. Everything was right, my little family developed splendidly, my wife helped in the company, what more did I want."

"But I think I was doing too well, there came a time in Italy when almost all companies went on strike and the economy came to a virtual standstill, delivery problems, poor quality, paid goods were not delivered, so a total mess. But the crowning glory of it all was, one of my best customers in Germany sold his company to a housing association, they had taken over everything and ordered me to their office on December 23. Since there were still open invoices, I thought they wanted to settle up and pay. The management said they only wanted to pay 50% of the outstanding invoices, if I didn't agree they would declare bankruptcy for this purchased company, then I would get nothing. A nice

Christmas present. We ended up having to declare bankruptcy because 2 other big customers got into trouble. I could no longer pay my debts. The crisis came everywhere. Now I had no income and my savings black I did not want to attack, especially since I would lose everything by the bankruptcy, but the saved was invested elsewhere and safe for me."

"To live, he took on various jobs that did not last long, but brought in money. So one day he met a gentleman who imported food, especially meat. He made Otto a good offer and then his wife also worked in this company."

"Since I had the opportunity and knowledge through my business studies to find out about this company and once I was alone in the office, I made a list of the life of this company. The result was, this company will not grow old. They were looking for new meat suppliers abroad and got the order to look for new suppliers of beef in South America, why shouldn't I take this trip that was paid for, even though I knew the company was not going to get old."

"Two weeks Paraguay, got to know the country and its people and traveled almost the entire country. I was traveling with a German who was building the telephone network for Telecom, and so I got to see a lot. The country inspired and back, I told my wife, I want to go to this country. Meanwhile, the company was almost ready to go bankrupt, and it didn't take two weeks before it filed for bankruptcy. I stayed in the office with my wife to wind up this company. The bailiff was the daily customer, and we could help wind up fairly.

"An old friend of mine, Harry was a sergeant major in the German Army, founded a summer camp for normal and thalidomide children in the Bavarian mountains. The children lived in the mountains for a few weeks, it was like an Indian camp, there were horses for the disabled children, and much more.

I had nothing to do and so my friend asked me, help out for a while. I agreed and with my wife, we started to help in the camp. We liked it and meanwhile they prepared everything for the emigration from Germany. (8 weeks we helped to make a nice time for the children, then the day of farewell came and many of the children had tears in their eyes). It was also not easy for us to part with the dear children.

How I emigrated

"Now we first went by car to Barcelona and on the ferry to Gran Canaria, we rented a bungalow and lived there for almost 2 years. The children went to the American school and learned English as well as Spanish. As fate would have it, I was at the airport in Las Palmas and bought the Frankfurter Allgemeine newspaper, it fell on the floor and I opened the advertising pages. There were many offers from Paraguay. I wanted to go there to see if there was anything for us. So, I flew to South America".

"I call it coincidence, the newspaper, the page that came first with the offers, then on the plane sitting next to me was a gentleman and as is so common we got to talking. He was a dentist from Frankfurt am Main and had land and cattle in Paraguay. Since I had no idea about this country, my seat neighbor was a good contact person

We then also stayed in the same hotel and there he introduced me to his friend, a German-Argentinean who had a wine factory. I was then invited to dinner by this gentleman, and we chatted. The South American friend of Hans the dentist, was named Julio and during the conversation he said that he had properties that he wanted to sell. He said it was 50,000 hectares, and he wanted to start a colony and sell it to German and also German Brazilians. Hans later asked me if I wasn't interested in buying a plot of land or marketing the project with Julio.

"My problem is, I'm always a bit hasty, and so I said to Julio, o.k., let's sell the land. But I had never done anything like this before, and later I thought, if only this goes well".

"Back in Gran Canaria I arranged my things there, I told my wife and told her I wanted to earn some money there and prepare everything so that you can follow me with the children". So, a new adventure began, and I flew back to Paraguay".

Paraguay, the future country

Coincidences played a big role in my life and here is another one. There was a German Jesuit priest who lived and worked in southern Brazil, he heard about our project and asked in a letter if we had land for sale for his community members because families in Brazil were large and people's lands were getting smaller and smaller because every child, when they got married, got a plot of land. On the other hand, land in Brazil was getting more and more expensive.

"So I answered the letter of Father Gruber (a Jesuit priest to whom Pope Pius had issued a letter with permission, he can work and preach anywhere in the world) Father Gruber was an excellent man with a difficult and painful life (he was imprisoned in a penal camp in Yugoslavia after the war, but did not want to be released until the last prisoner was released, on the Internet you can find his resume - Wendelin Gruber).

"So one day a message came from Father Gruber that a delegation from his parish would come and see the country. And they came, they came in a VW bus, over 20 people crammed in like herrings, and made the long trip of over 4000 km from Rio Grande do Sul to Paraguay. They were excited and we wrote the first contracts. The plots were all 20 hectares, people could buy as many plots as they wanted. After this visit, more and more German Brazilians came to buy plots, many stayed right away and started to build a house and cultivate the land. Then German buyers also came and settled there. Today it is a well-functioning colony, with a school, a church, a small hospital and of course a church. Father Gruber died in Rome in 2002."

Paraguay, which became his second home

"So I came to Paraguay, I said to myself *Otto, you are here now, and we want to start all over again and establish our second home here*, my family was still living in Gran Canaria. As with all business with me, it started to go well, Paraguay was very much in demand in Germany at that time, and today it is again. I also bought 400 hectares of land, located on a stream and rebuilt a cottage for me when I am on my land, can live and sleep."

"In Asunción, the capital, I rented a house, and I could have my family join me, the children went to the American school and a good life began for us. The circle of friends grew and there were many invitations. I had the best connections and was appreciated in this country. We lived in this house in Asunción for 3 years and felt comfortable."

"One day a new client came from Germany, and we visited the plots of the new colony, it was named Moseldorf. At the end we went to my plot. Meanwhile, I had also bought 30 young cattle with a bull and the customer asked me what I wanted for the farm. The offer this customer made me was such that I just couldn't say no and sold my farm of 400 hectares."

"That proves again, somehow everything works out the way you didn't think it would, but that price of the offer was flawless. We moved to the Brazilian border to a farm of 2000 hectares that I had sold a German, as a manager. It was a beautiful farmhouse there, and we lived in it for 2 years.

"One day an acquaintance in Brazilian part of the city, he had a trade in agricultural items, told me that a Japanese wanted to sell his finca of 60 hectares, we looked at everything and bought it."

"The farm grew vegetables and tomatoes in addition to soy, wheat and corn. All 4 of us moved to this farm and planted tomatoes and vegetables. Every day in the early morning the fruits were harvested and then immediately, driven to the nearest town and sold."

"It was a nice time, I knew the work, I had learned it once. The rest of the land I planted once with soybeans in the summer and in the winter corn and wheat."

"There was also a small piece, with bananas and with tangerines, there were many tree fruits on this small farm and 3 ponds for which we bought fish. This small farm had everything you can think of, chickens for eggs, rabbits for slaughter, ducks and also 2 geese. We baked our bread, it was delicious. And so, we lived almost independently as self-supporters.

"My two boys had many friends in the city and for the weekend they were always away and came back on Sunday evening. The closest neighbors from the farm of ours were 1 Japanese, 1 Brazilian 2 Paraguayans and some more, we exchanged, one had potatoes, we had tomatoes, the other had meat, one had milk, and so on. So, life was completely independent in the food sector. We often went to the city to visit good friends. So, it gave a good meaning to life".

"If there was a problem, we quickly found the solution. Water I had with a spring that gave the water for 3 ponds. Here we tapped to pump drinking water to an elevated tank to supply his house and 2 others. We had electricity through a windmill that stored electricity in batteries, so we had light and could watch local television."

There was no electricity and running water, we have taken a shower and most importantly, a flush toilet, it was the only one in a 10 km radius.

Otto told me; "he was always looking for danger and when an offer came from the government to go out with a pilot to plant marijuana in the vast forests, he accepted. For two years he flew with this pilot 1 x a week for 3 hours over the forests and photographed the plantations. The government then destroyed them with crop dusters.

"One day at night I had heard a voice in my sleep saying to me "get out of here as soon as possible, there is great danger", so I woke up my wife and told her. She said, order a truck from our friend tomorrow morning and we will start right now to pack and prepare everything we want to take with us. So it happened. I notified his friend and I called a friend in the capital, I told him everything and I asked him if there was a house for rent. The friend wanted to look around. When we started at noon, I received a message with the address of our new apartment. The truck started immediately, he had the new address, and then we followed with the car. They arrived the other morning, the truck was also there, and they unloaded everything and set up home. It was a nice house with a swimming pool, and it was nice to live there.

A week later I got the news that the pilot I was on the plane with had been shot. My wife told me the voice saved our lives. So, after his 10 years on the farm, we had started a new life once again.

What happened next in the capital

"I got bored with the time, all day in the house and I said I want to look for a job, so he came home in the evening and said I rented a well-known Pariliada, we open next week and start grilling meat. As it is usual with Otto, this business went excellent, they had many guests and the income was also excellent.

After 2 years, it was February 2, 1990, tanks were driving on the street in the evening, he thought it was a military exercise, and they had guests from the government, who suddenly paid quickly and disappeared and then many journalists came, they all wanted to make phone calls. It was the day of the revolution, in which the government was overthrown. We were open all night because new guests kept coming. When it became day, the whole spook was over. There was a new president and a new government. We opened again, but it wasn't the same.

"I had inherited the mill in the little village in Thuringia when I was a kid and so the obvious thing was, we'll go back, we'll have a roof over our heads, so I flew to Germany to lay claim to my inheritance because meanwhile all my relatives were not idle and had all filed their claim, everybody had inherited. However, there was a will available, from my grandfather, which was kept in the court, and was before the clerk, and so I could take over my property."

Meanwhile, what had happened in Paraguay?

Back to the small village in Thuringia

"So slowly all the businesses were getting back on track, but what it used to be, it wasn't anymore. In addition, there was theft and robbery, so we decided to cancel the lease because to work only for the cost, we did not want. What was to be done now, no more business and starting a new one held far too much risk. After my flight back to Paraguay, we settled everything there and then went back to Germany for good, my wife flew to Germany a month later. The children were married meanwhile and stayed in the country.

Germany, a new beginning

"Back in Germany, the old mill first had to be renovated to some extent because it was used by the young people in the village as a clubhouse, it was terribly dirty, windows were broken and the walls were smeared with black paint, with slogans of the former GDR. So I looked for a painter who could also renovate other things. Meanwhile, I had bought a van to bring in everything needed to renovate."

"So we made the old house habitable again to some extent,

I bought used furniture, we needed, kitchen, living room, bedroom and all the equipment to help us I bought a used washing machine, a refrigerator and a used television, so we could move in on November 1. It was already grimly cold, I had a tiled stove with oil heating built in the living room, so we could survive the winter well."

"I was no longer an emigrant nor a native and in the small village where I had grown up I was a stranger".

"Together with my wife we opened a small supermarket, which was also excellently used by the locals, but then a large shopping center came 20 km away, and the small supermarket was only visited for goods that had run out or were needed quickly. What was the conclusion: We had to close our store.

"My wife fell ill during this time and the doctors diagnosed colon cancer. She was operated on and then sent to rehab, came back home but after 3 months I had to call the paramedics again, and she was taken to the hospital again, then rehabilitation and from there straight back to the hospital. It was a horrible year for me. Every day drove a few 100 km to the hospital to visit my wife, but she did not recover and had to bury her in August."

"I was destroyed, and also didn't have much desire to live anymore, but as it was, I heard again that voice that saved my life once before, it said something like: "why are you so upset, why are you worrying, you have many problems right now. Why don't you send all your problems to the universe, let it help you"?

"The next morning I stood up, raised my head and said: "Dear God, I hereby hand over all my worries and problems to you, you do what you want with them, but leave me alone with them".

After that, I immediately felt much freer".

"I have a childhood friend, he was the last the friends left. He said to me one day Otto, I started a business, it's going great, and I'm earning well, I want to expand, but I don't have the money for this, help me". He showed him business papers, and they were promising".

"Since it was a large sum, I went to my bank and applied for a loan in the amount my friend wanted. As collateral, I gave my house and my fields (my inheritance) and so I could help the friend. It could not go wrong, my friend had given me insight into his books, and they were excellent, and I thought to myself, with this investment I have provided for my old age. I was satisfied, I could help my friend, and he will make nice money for me from now on."

"One day I received a letter from the bank, the friend had declared bankruptcy and the bank now wanted me to pay back the money. My friend didn't think it was necessary to tell me, his friend. That's how much a friendship is worth! Without payment, they will auction the collateral said the bank".

"I thought, doesn't it stop, whenever I start something new it goes great for a long time and I earn well, but then always somehow it ends, and I lose everything again, what is that?"

"Auctioning, I told myself is useless, and then I sit on the remaining debt, better is to sell everything, pay off the debt and maybe then there will be something left to start a new life. After I had fought a small war with the bank, the bank (the GDR was not yet completely out of people) would not allow me to sell, they wanted to auction. Perhaps a bank employee was also interested."

"After that was settled, I sold all my inheritance, paid my bank debts and I still had 50,000 marks left. With those, I wanted to start a new life again. Meanwhile, I was 65 years old and received a small pension. I said to myself, you can't live anywhere with this money, but the 50,000 will help me along. Then I received a notice from the pension insurance company that I was entitled to a widower's pension for my deceased wife. So it is possible with this money to start again in the Dominican Republic. We were there once on vacation years ago and we liked it very much, I think I can live there alone.

What happened with Otto?

Otto arrived there well and now lives in the Dominican Republic, he found a cheap house, and he bought it, or rented it for life, that is common in these countries. He has also found a partner again and is no longer alone.

Epilogue

In the year of Covid-19, this problem that Otto had has become even worse. Many have lost their jobs, business owners who had good going businesses have to declare bankruptcy, many lose their dearest partners, and also died from the virus, then comes the moment, what should I do now, they are lonely and for some the comforter alcohol helps, also drugs are common nowadays, to pay for that they cheat and steal. Others sit gloomily at home, have no other occupation than watching TV while drinking a bottle of beer.

Some had or have bought a dog to help them overcome their loneliness, it then becomes their constant companion and best friend. It becomes difficult for these people, they have no momentum anymore, no desire and life is a big problem for them.

If you analyze Otto's life, the positive is almost balanced with the negative. Otto is a stand-up guy, he often fell, but he always got back up, he had the courage. Respect.

Everything he started brought him good money for a while, but then the other side came, and he lost everything or at least a big part of it.

Maybe the universe is against him, but that can't be the case, it had saved his life. He has a large part of good positive thoughts and thus always received good beginnings with good income but somehow then in his thought process came the negative and the universe also delivered that, usually a little more. They can, if their thoughts are positive, also get everything positive. "Think positive and the universe will reward you" is the saying.

It is known, in today's time it is not easy to think only positive, when you see how everything breaks, how many lose their existence.

But Otto was always lucky in his life, every time he fell on his face, then he got up and had another idea, or it turned out that way, to decide his life for himself.

With Otto something always came in between, an excellent job in Italy, then strikes and an economic disaster, he had in most cases no fault, then the bankruptcy of his company, first brilliant business, then the brutal side, only 50% pay and at the same time still 2 other large customers went broke.

But he found a decent paying job again with the meat people and through that he got to know his future country. It all looks like coincidence, the newspaper with the ads, the seat neighbor on the plane, the German from Telecom who showed him a lot of the country, then Hans and Julio who made it possible for him to start a new job and earn money.

The night voice on the farm that saved his life, the restaurant that was doing well, then the revolution. In Germany, the supermarket, then the big shopping center. Then the biggest blow, the death of his wife, but then at night again that voice that advised him to give everything to the universe.

Then the hammer, his best friend double-crossed him, he lost all his inheritance, but some luck, the 50,000 that remained. Again and again comes a ray of hope.

Then, Otto flew one day to the Dominican Republic, he had chosen an address on the peninsula Samana on the Internet and there he is still today. If one of you also has such a problem, then do it like Otto.

Everything is regulated in life, the universe gives everyone what he asks for if his thoughts are like that: I am poor, can't I get some of all the wealth that is in the world? What will the universe do to him? It will make him even poorer, it will bring more poverty into his house. Therefore, negative in life just brings more negative.

If every day you start the day in a good mood and full of courage, thinking abundance and wealth, then in some way you will be rewarded by the universe.

You see it every day, the poor homeless person on the corner begging for a few pennies, he usually has nothing to eat, no shelter, but all these people live without a future. If they get some money, then they buy alcohol to numb themselves in misery. Every day we can see such people for whom there is no future, they sit on street corners and supermarket entrances. If you want to help them, buy them something to eat, or invite them to a hamburger in the nearest snack bar, it would do these people good.

Carlos   Mateo   Author

When I was born, there was a wartime atmosphere and a little later the 2nd World War began.

After my studies, agriculture, wholesale, business administration, I worked in various companies in Germany and Italy.

Then I emigrated with my family to South America. After more than 15 years back to Germany, there was a revolution and a change of power.

I wrote my first book in 1998, published it myself and sold it through my publishing house. The title "Alternative in cancer treatment", 400 copies were sold.

After my wife died, I emigrated to Tenerife for good. During the Corona crisis I started writing again. My last book "Lupita, Liege auf krummen Beinen" in German and A love on crooked legs, Lupita" a book in English about a little dog, the book is in color.

Imprint

Name: Carlos Mateo

Address: C/Mesaola2

ES 38530 Candelaria / Tenerife

ISBN: 9798504227528

E-mail: manotkur@gmail.com Tel: +34680633108 This work is protected by copyright. All rights, including those of translation, reprint and reproduction of the work or parts thereof, are reserved. No part of this work may be reproduced in any form (photocopy, microfilm or any other process) or processed, duplicated or distributed using electronic systems, including for the purposes of teaching, without the written permission of the publisher. The reproduction of common names, trade names, product designations, etc. in this work, even without special identification, does not justify the assumption that such names would be considered free in the sense of trademark and brand protection legislation and may therefore be used by anyone. Despite careful proofreading, errors may creep in. The author and publisher are therefore grateful for any comments in this regard. Any liability is excluded, all rights reserved.

Notes

Notes

www.ingramcontent.com/pod-product-compliance
Lightning Source LLC
Chambersburg PA
CBHW070437220526
45466CB00004B/1720